Research LInKS: Leadership, Innovation, Knowledge, and Skills in the 21st Century

by

Dr. Sherwin Jay Prado Palaspas

COPYRIGHT © 2022 Research LInKS: Leadership, Innovation, Knowledge, and Skills in the 21st Century

By Dr. Sherwin Jay Prado Palaspas

Edited by Marie Ezekiel
Graphic Artist: Princess de Vera
Cover Designer: Melvin Pumaras

ISBN:
Hardbound-978-621-470-196-4
Softbound/Paperback-978-621-470-197-1
Mobile/Kindle-978-621-470-198-8

Published in the Philippines by:
Poetry Planet Book Publishing House
Rosario, Pozorrubio, Pangasinan, Philippines
Contact No.: 09554960044
Email: maritesritumalta@gmail.com

What is triumph without our sources of inspiration?

What is the essence of being at the peak of success without acknowledging the people who lifted you up?

Therefore, I sincerely express my gratitude to these wonderful people in my life. This humble accomplishment is dedicated to you:

to my parents, Edwin and Rosalina, who are the winds beneath my wings, thank you for the warmth of your love and care;

to my sister Sheena, thank you for being my best buddy;

to my friends Mark Angelo and Jayson, thank you for the wonderful company and constant motivation;

to my colleagues at San Nicolas National High School, thank you for all your support;

and to our Almighty God, thank you for being my ultimate source of strength and inspiration.

SHERWIN JAY PRADO PALASPAS EdD
Author

The 21st Century has posed a lot of challenges to us. Will these challenges make or break us? The answer lies in our hands.

RESEARCH LInKS (Leadership, Innovation, Knowledge and Skills in the 21st Century) is anchored to empower Filipino research teachers in overcoming the challenges of teaching research subjects particularly in the Senior High School as embedded in the K-12 Curriculum.

The book features three significant chapters namely: Unveiling the World of Research; Research and Leadership; and Innovations in Research, which aims to equip readers particularly research teachers and students with both time-tested and modern insights, techniques, and strategies in the field of research. It enables them to creatively and effectively cope with the emerging challenges in the field of education.

Moreover, the book is being presented in a simple yet comprehensive manner in order for readers of different walks of life be able to internalize the concepts easily. Also, it is anchored to the values of leadership and innovation as essential aspects of the research process. It goes beyond just the knowledge and skills being learned for it even reaches to the very depths and soul of the research process.

Let us go back to the question: Will the challenges make or break us? Again, the answer is indeed in our hands. Why not flip the pages to know the answer? Yes, indulge yourself with this humble book. Create a link between you and this book. At the end of the day, it is research that will save us from the gutters of ignorance.

Welcome to the world of research! Enjoy reading!

SHERWIN JAY PRADO PALASPAS EdD
Author

There is always a ray of hope!

No matter how dark the times has been, there will always be a light of hope. Despite the sorrows, frustrations, and other negative effects of the pandemic, there are always be people who serve as beacons of inspiration.

Dr. Sherwin Jay Prado Palaspas is one of these beacons. His genuine love for research and selfless passion to the teaching profession never stopped even during these challenging times. His book **RESEARCH LInKS** (Leadership, Innovation, Knowledge and Skills in the 21st Century) is a signification of his compassion to both Filipino research teachers and learners. Coming up with such a creative, substantial, and inspiring book like this is a priceless thing.

With this book, I am looking forward to meet upskilled Filipino research teachers who are more creative and innovative. I am expecting to see research leaders who will set the bar higher in the field of research. I am hoping to witness a domino effect among research students of their genuine love and passion for research.

I commend Dr. Palaspas for working beyond expectations. His brilliant idea of incorporating the values of leadership and innovation in his book is a manifestation of his desire to uplift not only our love for research, but also our significant roles in nation building. Through research, we can lead with positive example.

Now, it is your turn. Read the book and be the next beacon of hope!

FLORENCE D. GANIR PhD
Dean
Vedasto J. Samonte School of Graduate Studies
Northwestern University
Laoag City, Philippines

TABLE OF CONTENTS

Chapter 1

Unveiling the World of Research

1. Research Defined and Interpreted

Education leads the human souls to what is best and making what is best out of them.
-John Ruskin

Research is one of the best intellectual possessions a person can have to be able to manage change on his way of life in accordance to the needs and demands of society. It is a widely recognized tool for solving man's various problems and for making life more colorful and convenient. It is what propels humanity fueled by curiosity.

1.1. Swindoll, 2012
"Research is a process of accumulating and scrutinizing information in order to perpetuate knowledge of a phenomenon under a study."

1.2. Faltado, 2016
"Research signifies finding the truth about ideas and problems which were in existence before in different perspectives."

1.3. Reyes, 2019
"The contribution towards the understanding of the phenomenon and delivering it to others is the aim of research as it gives rewarding learning experiences for students, producing graduates of high personal and professional achievement."

1.4. Cudapas, 2021

"Knowledge in doing research is an advantage for teachers not only for their professional development but also to improve research instructions. Hence, the culture of research must be developed within the school community so that teachers will view research as a part of the teaching and learning process, rather than just a simple requirement for career advancement."

1.5. Palaspas, 2021

"Research has turned into one of the most important rational assets for all human being to transform his way of life. Man's huge rise depends upon research which made a significant function in itself."

2. Importance of Research

Research does not simply set results and recommend actions. The importance of research should be measured on the extent to which they are being actually carried out. Taflinger (2011) cites two basic importance of research, to learn something or to gather evidence. To learn something is for the people's benefit. It is almost impossible for an individual to stop learning. Conducting research in an educational setting is important in every educator's life (Educational Research, 2011).

Education should look at research as a way to develop new understanding about teaching, learning, and educational administration based on gathered evidence. This new knowledge will lead to the improvement of educational practice (Gall and Brag as cited by Almeida, 2016). Through research results, new and innovative ideas were offered to solve education system problems; however, as days progress and society advance, problems add up and the demand for further research increases (Zhou, 2012).

To inform action is the primary purpose of research. Thus, research studies should seek to contextualize its findings within the larger body of research. In order to produce knowledge that is applicable outside of the research setting, research must always be of high quality. Furthermore, the results of researches may have implications for policy and future project implementation. The slow translation of research into practice is one problem that often plagues progress. Frequently, a disconnect happens between those who conduct research and those who are positioned to implement the research findings. The main problem is that "the production of evidence is organized institutionally with highly centralized mechanisms, whereas the application of that science is highly decentralized. Thus, as researchers, it is imperative to take steps to overcome this issue. Publishing research studies is one initial step to make it known to the global community. Other practical measures can be taken to encourage the acceptance of evidence-based interventions.

Well-conducted research is important to the achievement of global endeavors. Not only does research form the basis of program development and policies all over the world, but it can also be translated into effective global programs. Research obtains its power from the fact that it is empirical: rather than merely theorizing about what might be effective or what could work, researchers go out into the field and design studies that give legislators hard data on which they can base their decisions. Moreover, good research develops methodologies that can be replicated, produces results that are examinable by peers, and creates knowledge that can be applied to real-world situations. Researchers work as a team to enhance our knowledge of how to best address the world's problem (http://www.uniteforsight.org).

3. Research Education Curriculum in the K-12 Program

Philippine education is regarded as a pillar of national development and a primary avenue for social and economic mobility. The Filipino people have deep concern for education because it occupies a central place in political, economic, social, and cultural life in the Philippines. However, there are some significant issues that needs to be looked closely and resolved by the government. The quality of Philippine education has declined due to poor results from standard tests conducted among elementary and secondary students, as well as the tertiary levels. High dropout rates, high number of repeaters, low passing marks, lack of particular linguistic skills, congested classrooms, and poor teacher performances, have significantly affected the quality of education in the Philippines.

This notable decline in the achievement levels of students is alarming and discouraging, yet so challenging to note. These dismal results have been attributed to poor quality of education, scarcity of relevant and updated instructional materials, poor governance structures, fragmented school culture as well as school curriculum deficiency, teaching-learning dynamics, quality teacher training, and state-of-the-art equipment and facilities (Sleeter, 2008).

The implementation of the K to 12 Curriculum is one of the solutions that the Philippine government has looked up to for the reformation of quality education. It is the flagship program of the Department of Education (DepEd) in its desire to offer a curriculum that is attuned to the 21st century. This is in pursuance of the reform thrusts of the Basic Education Sector Reform Agenda, a package of policy reform that seeks to systematically improve critical regulatory, institutional, structural, financial, cultural, physical and informational conditions affecting education provision, access and delivery on the ground. The department seeks to create a basic education sector that is capable of attaining the country's Education for All objectives, Millennium Development Goals (MDGs), and the former president's Ten-point Basic Education Agenda.

The K to 12 Program comprises Kindergarten and 12 years of basic education to deliver sufficient time for mastery of concepts and skills, develop lifelong learners, and prepare graduates for tertiary education, middle-level skills development, employment, and entrepreneurship. Specifically, a 12-year program is expected to be the adequate period for learning under basic education and is a requirement recognition of professionals abroad following the Bologna and Washington Accords.

The Senior High School Curriculum has three groups of subjects/courses, namely: (1) core, (2) specialized, and (3) applied. Applied or contextualized subjects are subjects that all SHS students will take, however, contrary to core subjects which are only meant to cover the most basic of topics, applied subjects are designed to focus on the specific applications of certain subjects on the students' chosen career track or learning strand. Applied subjects under the research education curriculum of the SHS include Practical Research 1, Practical Research 2, and Inquiries, Investigation, and Immersion. These research subjects are required on all tracks and strands but must be taught in the context of the track. Meaning, all students are expected to acquire the learning competencies stipulated in the curriculum guide but the desired research outputs vary depending on the strand and track. These subjects aim to develop students' critical thinking and problem-solving skills through qualitative and quantitative researches. On the other hand, specialized subjects are subjects that are unique to the career track or learning strand that the student chose. Research Project/Capstone is one example of a specialized research subject in the STEM strand. This subject is similar to the major subjects that college student take, although they are designed to be less complex than their college counterpart.

Based from the DepEd Primer (2011), the said curriculum envisions holistically developed learners with 21st century skills. At the core of this basic education program is the complete human development of every graduate. This further means that every student would have an understanding of the world around him and a passion for a life-long learning, while addressing every student's basic learning needs – learning to learn, the acquisition of numeracy, literacy, and scientific and technological knowledge as applied to daily life. In addition, every graduate is envisioned to have respect for human rights and would aim to become *maka-Diyos, makatao, makabansa,* and *makakalikasan.*

In the 21st century, wherein everyone lives in a world of inquiry, the call for scientific activity has become explicit. In all endeavors whether academic, business, government, or social in nature, quality of services or outputs is demanded; hence, researches have to be conducted to promote continuous improvement (Andrew, 2015).

In the Philippines, recent efforts have been directed to improving research education, both at the basic and teacher education levels. Research shows that the quality of research education in schools is greatly influenced by the quality of research teachers. Students' interest in research is directly linked to the quality of teaching, as well as learning interactions provided by their research teachers. Interviews with students, who excel in research subjects, reveal that they are greatly inspired by their research teachers, who engage them in tasks that enable them to inquire and solve problems (Alda, 2020).

There are many constraints facing research education in Philippine schools. These include shortage of qualified research teachers, lack of quality textbooks, inadequate equipment, large classes, lack of support from administrators, and many others. However, the researcher decided that the framework for research teacher education should pay attention to problems that will address ways to improve or raise the quality of teaching practices, and personal attributes.

4. Problems Encountered by Research Teachers

Quality and relevant research education for national and international development is an urgent need of the country today. Upgrading it means a positive effect in the attainment of this goal. With the current status of our SHS Research Education Curriculum, there are the problems, issues, concerns, and challenges on its implementation.

Shortage of qualified research teachers. The shortage of qualified research teachers is one of the most prevalent problems in the implementation of the Research Education Curriculum in the SHS. Teachers are not given the chance to be prepared as well as to deal with students. Qualified research teachers are still lacking in the country based on the following reasons:

First, courses in college such as Bachelor in Elementary Education (BEEd) and Bachelor in Secondary Education (BSEd) only offer a three-unit subject in Research. Aside from that, action research was not required for graduating students.

Second, training programs were also given but they are shorter in duration and less intensive. Teachers who had undergone the training do not cascade or re-echo what they learned. They just use their certificates for promotion purposes.

Finally, the dwindling number of qualified research teachers is worsened by the brain drain phenomenon. Filipinos with master's and doctoral degrees are in demand overseas. In particular, industrialized countries have been aggressive and persistent in recruiting highly qualified Filipino teachers.

Incongruent teaching assignments with teachers' educational background. Lack of qualified research teachers in many schools leads to the practice of assigning teachers to teach research subjects inspite of their limited background. Based on researches, most of the teachers teaching research are science majors. When asked what topics do they find difficult to teach or students have difficulty in understanding the concepts, they included problem identification, statistical treatment, and interpretation of data. These topics require higher order thinking skills. Lacking in confidence to teach these topics, teachers tend to focus on topics they are familiar with and leave out the difficult ones. When teachers do not possess efficient knowledge and skills, then this may prove to be detrimental in enhancement of their careers as well as student learning. There have been instances, when teachers lack the information and are not able to respond to student queries, hence they encounter these problems, they may not be able to stay in the profession for a longer duration, hence they leave their jobs, resulting in the shortage of teachers.

Predominance of teacher-centered classrooms. Teaching research through the transmission approach is still predominant. In this approach, the teacher facilitates the learning and passes onto learners the knowledge and skills, treating them as empty vessels which the teacher fills. There is an evidence of transmission approach to learning especially in secondary school, may be contributing to the lack of interest in research that is now widespread among secondary school student across the country. The low percentage of doing good researches in tertiary education can be attributed to the poor quality of research teaching in many Philippine secondary schools.

Learner-centered classes have been found effective in enhancing students' critical and creative thinking skills. The approach is anchored on the philosophy that students learn best when they hear, see, and manipulate variables (also referred to as interactive learning). Consequently, the method by which learning occurs is oftentimes based on actual experiences. For many years, training programs zeroed in on the utilization of practical work approach (PWA) to teaching and learning. This approach requires teachers to use hands-on and minds-on activities to stimulate students' curiosity and imagination. In a learner-centered classroom, the teacher's role is to facilitate intellectual growth by utilizing the interest and exceptional needs of students as a guide to meaningful learning. Students' learning is then evaluated based on predetermined and developmentally-oriented objectives.

Sadly, teacher-centered classes can still be observed in many Philippine schools. Lacking in content and pedagogical skills suitable for research teaching, many research teachers turn to lecturing instead of providing students with engaging and challenging activities that enable the latter to develop creative ideas.

Further, assessment of student learning is still predominantly at the factual knowledge level. Sample tests reviewed attest to this. Use of open-ended questions is not common. The outcome of the assessment is not used to improve teaching. It has to be recognized that what gets assessed is what gets learned and good assessment translates to good teaching.

Lack of textbooks and other equipment. The K-12 Curriculum started in the year 2013. Up to now, there were no books published and distributed for Practical Research subjects. As a result, teachers download reference materials from the internet or buy reference books in bookstores. More often than not, teachers tend to mimic what is written on the reference books instead of explaining the concepts in depth vis-a-vis their applications and connections to real life situations. Research subjects are output-based but most schools do not still have computers or printers to be used by the students. For quantitative researches, doing investigatory projects is an example. It cannot be properly done due to lack of laboratories, science apparatus, and reagents (Reyes, 2019).

Lack of Time. For most of the research teachers, time is the reason why the development of research culture among them is low (Firdissa, 2015). This is because teachers use most of their time in teaching, preparing lessons, checking papers, recording, and computing grades. He stressed that if there is a little time left for them to meet their personal needs. If the timetables of these teachers are not loosened, they would not prioritize research as their main job responsibility (Ellis and Loughland, 2016). Similarly, in the study of Mergler and Spooner (2012), among the predominantly undergraduate institutions in the United States of America had concluded that time is the limiting factor in conducting research since more time is devoted to teaching. Teachers devote more time to the teaching of lessons, checking papers, recording and computing grades at the same time balancing with research activities and community services.

Garcia (2011) as cited by Natividad (2018) stressed that lack of time is the main reason why teachers are not performing much on research. She emphasized that the complex nature of teaching, pressures, and tension attached to the profession are often some of the complaints in time management issues. The teaching loads of teachers would affect the time in doing researches. As what Kho and Ling (2017) said, teachers who have higher teaching load aside from the student-teacher ratio, minimize their research productivity and other scholarly activities. Thus, in order to upgrade their skills, development programs must be intensively implemented.

Lack of Fund. In terms of the budget, only a portion of school fund is allotted since there are other more important needs to be purchased in public schools such as medicines, bond papers, and the like. Many articulated the difficulty of getting research funding and support for paper presentations especially for international conferences. Considering that much of the operations budget of schools, 90% goes to teaching salaries, it is no wonder why limited funds go to research (Gonzales, 2006 as cited by Salazar, et.al., 2020).

Chapter 2

Leadership and Research

1. Empowering Research Teachers as Nation Builders

Pursuant to DepEd Order No. 001, s. 2020 titled Guidelines for National Educators Academy of the Philippines (NEAP) Recognition of Professional Development Programs and Courses for Teachers and School Leaders, the DepEd, through the NEAP, issues the DepEd Professional Development Priorities for Teachers and School Leaders for School Year 2020-2023. It shall support the realization of the Department's goal of continuous upskilling and reskilling of teachers and school leaders that will result in better learning outcomes.

Researchers long have recognized that teachers' professional development is indispensable to changing classroom practice, improving schools, and ameliorating pupils' learning outcomes (Borko, 2004). Professional learning frequently takes place in formal settings, such as professional development programmes, teaching research groups, and formal mentoring programmes (Timperley, 2011). Teachers also can learn through informal interactions that happen during peer teaching, collaborative planning, and mentoring between colleagues (Little, 2012). Fullan (2007) posits that professional learning in context is the only education that ultimately changes classroom. Moreover, there is strong evidence that professional development is best when embedded in the teachers' specific subject areas (Darling-Hammond, et.al., 2009). Meanwhile, schools with strong teacher communities seem to have higher student achievement (Bryk, et.al., 2010)

Many presume that teacher collaboration contributes to professional development and instructional improvement (DuFour and Fullan, 2012). Research on teachers' professional development also indicates that site-based teacher teams positively influence teacher engagement in terms of new instructional practices (Garet, et.al., 2001). According to Borko (2004), participation and discourse practices can improve teacher learning by supporting professional critique, reflection, and collaboration. However, research also shows that many schools and teacher educators struggle to foster constructive interactions. Research further emphasizes that openness in expressing disagreement is important for constructive dialogue and learning in teacher collaboration (Dobie and Anderson, 2015).

The lesson study (LS) method is one of the widely used collaborative models for teachers. A lesson study cycle starts with teachers working with an established common objective, along with a series of lesson planning sessions culminating in the enactment and observation of the research lessons. The different phases of LS serve as a key part of the practice architecture or the preconditions affecting how LS has been enacted in classrooms and schools. According to LS, the goal setting for the pupils' learning and development should be aligned with the school's development goals (Lewis, et.al., 2013).

There is an important caveat to be addressed: despite the increasing popularity of collaborative models, the associated changes in teaching are often subtle, and dramatic changes are rare (Ermeling and Yarbo, 2016). One reason for this nuance is that teachers construct visions of classroom practice based on deeply rooted cultural routines and preconceived notions of effective and ineffective teaching (Stigler and Hiebert as cited by Andrew (2015). The teachers are constrained by their "horizons of observation" (Hutchins as cited by Reyes, 2019) and may need outside experts to expand their visions of what is possible. These outside experts can be local scientists, researchers, or university faculty (Ermeling and Yarbo, 2016).

Studies also show that teachers can be development leaders in their own schools. For instance, Alexandrou and Swaffield (2014) demonstrate that teacher leadership can facilitate comprehensive professional development within school communities. MacBeath and Dempster (2008) show five principles for teacher leaders in their work: First, they should focus on the learning of everyone in the school. Second, they should create and sustain conditions that favor learning. Third, they should join in explicit, transparent, and inquiry-based dialogue. Fourth, they should permit everyone to influence school operations; and fifth and finally, they should sustain internal and external accountability in order to examine how the results align with their school's goals and principles. Of course, there also are some conditions that allow teacher leadership to flourish, including professional trust, perceived autonomy, supportive administrators, and time and resources, such as structural and organizational assets along with space and time (Birky, et.al., 2006).

Another professional development for teachers is the conduct of the weekly Learning Action Cell for teachers in the Philippines. As stated in DepEd Order No. 35, s. 2016, Learning Action Cell (LAC) is a session held by group of teachers who participate in collaborative learning sessions to solve shared challenges encountered in school. Such challenges may consist of learner diversity and student inclusion, content and pedagogy, assessment and reporting, and 21st century skills and ICT integration. DepEd envisions that these LAC Sessions will serve as a school-based continuing professional development strategy for the enhancement of teaching and learning. The development of the culture of research is one of the primary aims of the Department of Education. Thus, one of the topics during these sessions focused on research.

With all these being said, empowering Filipino research teachers is a way of preparing them to be nation builders.

2. The Research Competencies Framework

Gray (2007), the chair of the Faculty of General Dental Practice (United Kingdom) Research Committee initiated the creation of the Research Competencies Framework based on the following objectives: (1) describe the competencies (knowledge, skills and learning outcomes) required in the different aspects of research relevant to primary oral healthcare; (2) list suggested learning and assessment methods relevant to each competency; (3) list existing Faculty training material and references relevant to the competencies; and (4) demonstrate that the Faculty has an ongoing commitment to the development of evidence-informed primary oral healthcare, and to research in this area. This is to ensure that all Faculty members (and all other oral healthcare providers) should be competent in critical appraisal of the scientific literature relevant to their practice, and that some will have the ability to apply research in primary care settings, such as their practices.

The basis for the framework for the research competencies utilizes an evolutionary model. An individual entering the Career Pathway will previously have gained an array of competencies of varying levels, some of which have significance to research. The preliminary phase is therefore to map the individual's existing competencies against those defined in the curriculum of competencies for research, and then highlight those that may need to be developed.

Individuals will have developed some competencies during their college studies. The framework is intended to help them identify, and where necessary achieve, a higher level of competence in some areas, and/or acquire new competencies in other areas.

Within the framework, its five domains include aspects pertinent to research. Each part is sub-divided into more detailed areas of competence. A description is given of the training activities that can be undertaken to enable individuals to realize each competency.

In future, within health and oral healthcare, it is expected that an employer will recognize the areas and levels of competency that any prospective employee will need, to assure that they can achieve the requirements of the job/post concerned. In an era of evidence-informed practice, all those working in healthcare will need some of the competencies identified.

Gray (2007) grouped the research competencies into five domains. They are: (1) Practical skills; (2) Problem-solving, thinking and communication skills; (3) Personal attitudes and professional ethics; (4) Dissemination; and (5) Roles and functions.

The foundation for the selection of these topics is grounded on three concepts. The first is the step-by-step process of the scientific method, specifically the identification of a problem; the formation of a hypothesis; deductive reasoning, data collection and analysis; and the derivation of a conclusion. The second is the utilization of a framework using the concepts of structure, process and outcome to complete the scientific method and the adoption of current good practice. The third is the relevance of dissemination, and the skills required to create a research paper.

Domain A – Practical Skills. This domain is divided into five competencies. They are: (1) find and use resources; (2) use library and information technology effectively; (3) recognize and know when to use primary and secondary resources; (4) observe and record behavior; and (5) demonstrate basic computer competency.

Domain B – Problem-Solving, Thinking, and Communication Skills. This domain is divided into five competencies that deal with the individual's ability to critique, communicate, and identify shortfalls in existing information. They are the ability to: (1) understand the difference between subjective and objective information; (2) recognize when information provided is sufficient; (3) evaluate when the basis for conclusions is laid out completely and clearly; (4) generate research questions by recognizing gaps in knowledge; (5) use oral and written communication to express ideas effectively.

Domain C – Personal Attitudes and Professional Ethics. This domain is divided into three competencies that cover personal attitudes and professional ethics. The competencies are the ability to: (1) demonstrate an appreciation of the necessity and value of research for competent clinical practice; (2) demonstrate an awareness and adherence of ethical principles underpinning research, in particular those produced by the Department of Health; (3) design and implement research studies that evaluate clinical practice and service delivery.

Domain D – Dissemination. This domain is divided into two competencies which deal with the dissemination of research findings and the ability to influence clinical practice. They are: (1) demonstrate the skills required for publication of research reports; and (2) change clinical practice based on outcome studies and other research.

Domain E – Roles and Functions. This domain is divided into six competencies. They are to: (1) engage in activities that contribute to the development of a body of knowledge relevant to health and oral healthcare; (2) design and implement a series of studies that address a significant issue; (3) write research funding applications to major funding bodies; (4) offer help and support to other researchers; (5) publish in major journals, both dental and non-dental.

3. Research Competence of Teachers

Research is one of the most challenging subjects in the secondary schools. Thus, teachers must be competent not only in teaching the subject but in the application of the research ethics as well. Hoeschl, et.al. (2017) specified that ethics is very important in conducting research. Several studies had been made to determine the research competencies of the teachers around the world. Gomez and Panaligan (2013) found out that teachers are competent in finding resources, conceptualizing research literature, and doing literature reviews but they still need to be trained to develop their writing skills to be more confident in doing research activities.

On the other hand, Efron and Ravid (2012) said that teachers do not have sufficient research skills and do not trust their ability to collect, discuss, evaluate, or interpret data. This is in consonance with the study of Pati (2014) that the difficulty of formulating the research question is a challenge that teacher-researchers face in the early stages of the action research process. The study of Kho and Ling (2017) showed that teachers are not so familiar with the contents and formats, particularly on grammar and sentence construction, research organization, and communication skills as well as other parts of the research process as associated with developing research findings. The survey conducted by the Department of Education in 2010 agrees with this result. It was found that 80 percent of secondary school teachers in the Philippines failed an English proficiency exam (Nolasco, 2010). Aside from that, the study of Magpayo (2015) reveals that teachers have average grammatical competence. The research of Garcia (2011) as cited by Natividad (2018) explained that teacher have fear and rigidity in conducting and teaching research. He also added that teachers do not trust their research knowledge and skills which is one of the factors why they restrain themselves from engaging in research.

Information and Communication Technologies (ICTs) are clearly of great significance for education. In our society where knowledge is increasing rapidly, teaching is becoming one of the most challenging professions. Modern developments have provided new opportunities to teaching professions but at the same time have placed more demands on teachers to learn how to use these new technologies in their teaching. With this, the findings of Alda (2020) suggest that faculty members perceived that they are ready in terms of their skills in selecting and integrating digital resources for teaching and learning as they are also given capacity buildings through seminars and conferences associated to technological literacy. He also pointed out that the use of digital tools and digital platforms is no longer an option but a way of life, it becomes a necessity for educational institutions to prepare, embrace, and apply these changes.

On the contrary, there are also teachers who are left behind. According to Alkhahtani (2017), one of the issues arising from ICT integration is the need to provide appropriate training that focuses on the operation of the ICT equipment and applications on the curriculum. The use of statistics coupled with technology is also one of the great challenges. Teachers need to be competent in developing a research design and determining the appropriate statistical tool for the teachers to do their research undertaking (Gomez and Panaligan, 2013).

In the realm of research teaching, collaboration and partnership among the external stakeholders should be conducted. Schartz and Sadler (2019) emphasized that research teachers need outside support and scaffolding to ensure that they operate at their optimal skills levels. The teachers are controlled by their "horizons of observation" and may need outside experts to expand their visions of what is possible (Hutchins as cited by Reyes, 2019).

Confidence in mentoring colleagues and learners affects research outcomes. Providing high-quality mentors to teachers yields major academic benefits for students (Terada, 2017). But in the study conducted by Ortal and Natividad (2018), Master Teachers have their lowest rating in providing technical assistance to other teachers of the teaching staff.

Aside from that, only few research teachers published their scholarly works. Wa-Mbaleka (2015) pointed out that little visibility of Filipino researchers on the international arena of scholarly publications can be observed. He further enumerated the factors that affect limited publications of research teachers such as limited time, lack of training, fear of rejection, lack of interest in writing and research, laziness, lack of funds, and lack of institutional support. Sali-ot (2019) emphasized that research and publication in the Philippines in recent years is consistently low. There was a minimal conduct of institutional researches for program improvement, publications in journal/peer reviewed creative works, research journal publication, presentations or demo teaching in local/national and/or international arena, and conduct of collaborative studies across colleges among others.

According to Luff and Hewson (2014), when teachers disseminate their works collaboratively in a professional learning community, they reinforce, build, expand, and challenge their notions about teaching research. But research dissemination is a major problem among research teachers especially in the Philippines. Teachers and master teachers are incapable in research dissemination suggesting that their capability is indeed low and would explain the reason for non-progressive research productivity (Wong, 2019).

4. Upskilling the Research Teacher

In the fast-paced world like today's, upskilling and reskilling have become buzzwords. Upskilling is defined as learning new skills and enhancing competencies. In simple terms, upskilling is training individuals in the same occupation, but in new way. On the other hand, reskilling is training individuals who have shown they have the aptitude to learn in a completely new occupation. The technological advancement and the emergence of artificial intelligence have made skill enhancement inevitable so as to be at par with the acceptable global standard. The Department of Education are investing heavily on their employees most especially the teachers to upskill and reskill them so as to increase productivity and survive in high competition.

Planning is key to an effective upskilling/reskilling program. It is vital to set the strategic direction; identify the skill gaps; conduct workforce analysis; develop and implement action plans; monitor and evaluate the performance of the programs; and develop and communicate an upskilling/reskilling strategy. Some key factors to ensure effective upskilling/reskilling are: (a) *leadership support*; (b) *appropriate resources*; (c) *workforce plans*; and (d) *policies to support upskilling/reskilling*.

The Implementation phase involves the identification of strategies to close gaps, plans to implement the strategies, and measures for assessing strategic progress. It also involves communicating progress and strategies on a regular basis. This phase involves mentoring programs, coaching programs, rotation opportunities, details training, shadowing programs, blended learning, online training, and career paths.

Andriotis (2017) cited different ways on how to implement upskilling/reskilling programs: (a) *Classroom Training.* Trainers can conduct classes in a classroom setting, allowing employees to learn new skills or enhance current ones. Trainers can present new ideas, allow participants to brainstorm and share ideas, use training software and bring trainees up to speed quickly. (b) *Virtual Classroom Training.* Investing in virtual classroom programs allows employees to upskill/reskill regardless of their location. Employees simply log in to the platform at the designated time and the facilitator can cover an abundance of upskilling/reskilling training topics. (c) *Microlearning.* Another effective way of upskilling/reskilling employee is to create web-based microlearning units, short web-based training modules that cover a topic in 5-10 minutes. Employees could improve their skills during short workday breaks by taking the microlearning units that interest them. (d) *Lunch and Learns.* Facilitators schedule a lunchtime training session to cover a certain topic over a complimentary meal, in a convivial and more relaxed atmosphere. Lunch and Learns can even be conducted online via Skype. Facilitators can share upskilling/reskilling presentations with the attendees while they eat at their desk. (e) *Mentors / Subject Matter Experts.* Employers offer their top producers an opportunity to develop their own leadership skills by mentoring others. Evaluation is an important step in all training programs. It begins at the design phase and continues beyond implementation. To assess the effectiveness of training and the impact on an employee's development for reskilling or closing a skill gap, evaluation must occur to gauge the impact and show measurable results. Evaluation data enables judgments about the following questions: (a) How well did the training meet the development needs identified? (b) How well did the learners master the training content? (c) How well did the learning transfer to the work setting? and (d) How well did the training contribute to the achievement of the agency's mission?

Training and development are tools that help increase workforce knowledge and ability in specific areas and lead to improvement in individual and organizational performance.

Chapter 3

Innovations in Research

1.Upskilling Program for SHS Research Teachers

Education leads the human souls to what is best and making what is best out of them (Ruskin as cited by Reyes, 2018). Thus, the goal of education is to bring out the best in every human being – that man is prepared to master himself and his environment in order to function effectively, achieve goals for himself, and make right actions and decisions in facing the challenges of the globally-competitive community.

Access to quality education is the first step to achieving a bright future. In the Philippines, every Filipino is accorded the right to enjoy and avail of access to quality basic education. While the country is experiencing numerous forms of development, the government is aggressively responding to the biggest lingering challenge of basic education, quality, particularly on students' learning outcomes. The Department of Education's *Sulong Edukalidad* is an educational reform program aimed at achieving quality in basic education. The initiative is in response to the rapidly changing learning environment of present and future learners and will introduce aggressive reforms to globalize the quality of basic education in the Philippines. It aims to focus on four key areas: (1) K to 12 Review and Updating; (2) Improvement of Learning Facilities; (3) Teacher and School Heads' Upskilling and Reskilling Through a Transformed Professional Development Program, and (4) Engagement of All Stakeholders for Support and Collaboration. Upskilling of teachers and school leaders which is one of the key areas paves the way to the attainment of quality education.
Teaching requires continuous innovation especially in the field of research. Research has turned into one of the most significant

rational assets for all human being to transform his way of life. Man's huge rise depends upon research which made an important function in itself. In the Philippines, the demands for research in education were addressed through the immersing pioneers of senior high school programs since 2016 until now.

With the fast-changing standards of quality education, teachers should be the champions in blazing a trail in keeping with uncertainties and reforms of educational landscape. The battle for quality research education is fought and won inside the classroom by the teachers. By investing and giving full support to educators for their in-service professional development, they will amplify their teaching competencies and skills. Thus, there is a need for an Upskilling Program for Senior High School Teachers (SHS) as they advance to their professional development.

This Upskilling Program was formulated based on the study conducted by the proponent on SHS teachers personal and professional characteristics, level of competence of the research teachers along practical skills based on the standard format prescribed by the education sector; problem-solving, thinking, and communication skills; personal attitudes and professional ethics; and researchers' roles and functions; and the problems they encountered in teaching the research subjects. Considering the gray areas with low ratings, appropriate measures to intensify skills and competencies of teachers were taken into account. This implies the necessity of upgrading their performance, competencies, and skills in order to facilitate more effective and efficient teaching-learning process.

Objectives of the Upskilling Program

This Upskilling Program was crafted to provide a blueprint to level up the skills, competence, and mastery of SHS teachers in implementing the research education curriculum. It was designed to assist teachers in making in-depth analysis of their own practices as they aspire for personal growth and professional development focused towards achieving the department's vision, mission, values, and strategic priorities in delivering quality educational services to Filipino learners.

Its main objective is to deliver strategic interventions in equipping SHS research teachers with up-to-date skills, adequate knowledge, and thorough understanding on how to teach research subjects. Likewise, it offers activities that will upgrade their content knowledge and pedagogical skills in meeting the needs of the learners.

Components of the Upskilling Program

The following components of the Upskilling Program were considered: (1) areas of concern; (2) objectives; (3) strategies; (4) persons and agencies involved; (5) time frame; (6) budgetary requirements; and (7) expected outcomes.

Areas of Concern. These pertain to the identified competencies and skills in which SHS research teachers need to intensify.

Objectives. These are the specific targets that SHS research teachers aim to achieve within a time frame using available resources.

Strategies. These are the specific activities that are to be undertaken by the persons or agencies involved in order to realize the different objectives set.

Persons and Agencies Involved. These include the human resources and entities involved in the implementation of the framework.

Time Frame. It specifies the month, year, and length of time to bring about the strategies/activities to be taken up in order to produce the expected outcomes.

Budgetary Requirements. It is the fund allocation to execute and realize the activities designed in the program.

Expected Outcomes. These are the results desired to be achieved after the implementation of the various activities covered in the Upskilling Program.

UPSKILLING PROGRAM FOR SENIOR HIGH SCHOOL RESEARCH TEACHERS

Areas of Concern	Objectives	Strategies	Persons and Agencies Involved	Time Frame	Budgetary Requirements	Expected Outcomes
A. Teaching Competencies and Skills ***1. Practical Skills***	To harness the practical skills of research teachers in terms of finding and using resources	Provide in-service trainings to SHS research teachers on topics focusing on finding and using resources Initiate a seminar on Learning Resource Management Conduct Learning Action Cell (LAC) Sessions on technical writing Hold Focus Group Discussions on Research Advising and Mentoring	SHS Research Teachers, School Heads, Department Heads Resource Speakers, Learning Resource (LR) Focal Persons, ICT Coordinators, Librarians	YEAR 1 J F M A M J J A S O N D	Php 50,000.00 Source of Fund: MOOE / Canteen Fund	80 – 100% of the SHS research teachers shall have attended trainings that will enable them to improve their skills in finding and using resources.
	To encourage teachers to utilize available resources in the library as well as enormous information which technology offers	Provide in-service trainings to SHS research teachers on the library and IT usage	SHS Research Teachers, School Heads, Department Heads Resource Speakers, Learning Resource	YEAR 1 J F M A M J J A S O N D	Php 10,000.00 Source of Fund: MOOE / Canteen Fund	80 – 100% of the SHS research teachers shall have been oriented and trained on the use of the library and IT resources.

Areas of Concern	Objectives	Strategies	Persons and Agencies Involved	Time Frame	Budgetary Requirements	Expected Outcomes
		Conduct Learning Action Cell (LAC) on the research process Initiate an orientation activity on how to use the library and other library resources	(LR) Focal Persons, Librarians			
	To deepen awareness and understanding of teachers on the use of primary and secondary resources	Participate in research seminars and workshops on interpreting source materials Conduct Learning Action Cell (LAC) on the research process	SHS Research Teachers, School Heads, Department Heads Resource Speakers	YEAR ROUND J F M A M J J A S O N D	Php 10,000.00 Source of Fund: MOOE / Canteen Fund	80 – 100% of the SHS research teachers shall have participated in research seminars and LAC sessions on interpreting source materials.
	To guide teachers on how to observe and record behaviors properly	Participate in research seminars and workshops on the different instruments used in observing and recording behaviors Conduct Learning Action Cell (LAC) on the research process	SHS Research Teachers, School Heads, Department Heads Resource Speakers	YEAR ROUND J F M A M J J A S O N D	Php 10,000.00 Source of Fund: MOOE / Canteen Fund	80 – 100% of the SHS research teachers shall have participated in research seminars and LAC sessions.

Areas of Concern	Objectives	Strategies	Persons and Agencies Involved	Time Frame	Budgetary Requirements	Expected Outcomes
	To assist teachers in acquiring basic computer literacy	Hold face-to-face or virtual computer literacy training Initiate in-service training on the use of statistical packages Conduct Learning Action Cell (LAC) Sessions on the use of technology in the teaching-learning process	SHS Research Teachers, School Heads, Department Heads, Resource Speakers, ICT Coordinators	YEAR 1 J F M A M J J A S O N D	Php 50,000.00 Source of Fund: MOOE / Canteen Fund	80 – 100% of the SHS research teachers shall have attended trainings on basic computer literacy.
2. ***Problem-Solving, Thinking, and Communication Skills***	To increase the level of understanding of teachers in using subjective and objective information	Conduct Learning Action Cell (LAC) Sessions on the research process	SHS Research Teachers, School Heads, Department Heads Resource Speakers	YEAR 1 J F M A M J J A S O N D	Php 5,000.00 Source of Fund: Canteen Fund	80 – 100% of the SHS research teachers shall have participated in LAC sessions in understanding the difference between subjective and objective information.
	To hone the skills of teachers in statistical concept and application to data collected	Conduct a seminar on the application of statistics to research Initiate in-service training on the use of statistical package	SHS Research Teachers, School Heads, Department Heads Resource Speakers	YEAR 1 J F M A M J J A S O N D	Php 10,000.00 Source of Fund: MOOE / Canteen Fund	80 – 100% of the SHS research teachers shall have participated in seminars and LAC sessions in the application of statistical packages in research.

Areas of Concern	Objectives	Strategies	Persons and Agencies Involved	Time Frame	Budgetary Requirements	Expected Outcomes
		Hold Focus Group Discussions on Research Advising and Mentoring especially on the statistical parts				
	To level up the knowledge of teachers in formulating research tools and interpreting and evaluating research results	Conduct seminars in Making Research Instruments and Interpreting Research Results	SHS Research Teachers, School Heads, Department Heads Resource Speakers	YEAR 1 J F M A M J J A S O N D	Php 10,000.00 Source of Fund: MOOE / Canteen Fund	80 – 100% of the SHS research teachers shall have participated seminars in making questionnaires and interpreting research results.
	To equip teachers' skills in generating research problems	Conduct Learning Action Cell (LAC) Sessions on the research process	SHS Research Teachers, School Heads, Department Heads Resource Speakers	YEAR ROUND J F M A M J J A S O N D	Php 5,000.00 Source of Fund: Canteen Fund	80 – 100% of the SHS research teachers shall have participated in LAC sessions in generating research questions.
	To amplify oral and written communication skills of teachers	Hold Brainstorming Sessions on Coaching Coordinate with the ICT department a training on Presentation of Data using Different Computer Applications Conduct seminars on Technical Writing	SHS Research Teachers, School Heads, Department Heads Resource Speakers	YEAR 2 J F M A M J J A S O N D	Php 10,000.00 Source of Fund: MOOE / Canteen Fund	80 – 100% of the SHS research teachers shall have participated in training on the presentation of data using different computer applications and technical writing.

Areas of Concern	Objectives	Strategies	Persons and Agencies Involved	Time Frame	Budgetary Requirements	Expected Outcomes
3. ***Personal Attitudes and Professional Ethics***	To equip teachers with ethical principles on research as well as their personal qualities on how to engage in research properly	Establish connections/tie-up with research organizations Sponsor membership fees of research teachers to encourage membership in professional research organizations Establish a school-based organization for research teachers where they can have the opportunity to share ideas and work together to enhance their self-assessments	SHS Research Teachers, Resource Speakers, School Heads, Department Heads, Heads of Research Education Institutions	YEAR 2 J F M A M J J A S O N D	Php 5,000.00 Source of Fund: Canteen Fund	80 – 100% of the SHS research teachers shall have established tie-up with research organizations to improve research instructions
		Conduct Learning Action Cell (LAC) Sessions on the different ethical principles in doing researches	SHS Research Teachers, School Heads, Department Heads Resource Speakers	YEAR 2 J F M A M J J A S O N D	Php 5,000.00 Source of Fund: Canteen Fund	80 – 100% of the SHS research teachers shall have participated in LAC Sessions on the different ethical principles in doing researches.

Areas of Concern	Objectives	Strategies	Persons and Agencies Involved	Time Frame	Budgetary Requirements	Expected Outcomes
	To improve research teachers' ability to design and utilize research studies	Conduct Learning Action Cell (LAC) Sessions on the research process	SHS Research Teachers, School Heads, Department Heads Resource Speakers	YEAR 1 (J F M A M J / J A S O N D)	Php 5,000.00 Source of Fund: Canteen Fund	80 – 100% of the SHS research teachers shall have participated in LAC Sessions on implementing and designing research studies.
4. Researchers' Role and Function	To strengthen awareness and sense of responsibility of teachers on their functions and roles in implementing the value of research	Encourage all research teachers to conduct personal researches Establish connections/tie-up with research organizations Create links with research publications Conduct seminars on how to publish research works	SHS Research Teachers, Resource Speakers, School Heads, Department Heads, Heads of Funding Agencies, Heads of Public and Private Publication Companies, Heads of Research Education Institutions, SDS, ASDS, Chiefs of CID and SGOD	YEAR ROUND (J F M A M J / J A S O N D)	Php 10,000.00 Source of Fund: MOOE / Canteen Fund	80 – 100% of the SHS research teachers shall have been enriched with activities that will contribute to the development of research.
	To guide teachers in doing research studies	Conduct Learning Action Cell (LAC) Sessions on the research process	SHS Research Teachers, School Heads, Department Heads Resource Speakers	YEAR ROUND (J F M A M J / J A S O N D)	Php 15,000.00 Source of Fund: Canteen Fund	80 – 100% of the SHS research teachers shall have been guided in doing research studies.

Areas of Concern	Objectives	Strategies	Persons and Agencies Involved	Time Frame	Budgetary Requirements	Expected Outcomes
		Conduct benchmarking activities or fieldtrips in institutions which are Center of Excellence along research				
	To encourage and assist teachers in sourcing out funds for research undertakings	Create links with research publications Conduct seminars on how to publish research works. Establish connections/tie-up with research organizations Encourage all research teachers to conduct personal researches Avail of the Basic Education Research Fund (BERF) program of the Department of Education (DepEd)	SHS Research Teachers, Resource Speakers, School Heads, Department Heads, Heads of Funding Agencies, Heads of Public and Private Publication Companies, Heads of Research Education Institutions, SDS, ASDS, Chiefs of CID and SGOD, Alumni	YEAR 3 J F M A M J J A S O N D	Php 75,000.00 Source of Fund: MOOE / Canteen Fund / Basic Education Research Fund	75% of the SHS research teachers shall have applied for research funding

Areas of Concern	Objectives	Strategies	Persons and Agencies Involved	Time Frame	Budgetary Requirements	Expected Outcomes
	To recalibrate the research teachers' competency in determining the appropriate research methodologies	Provide in-service trainings on the different strategies, techniques, and methods in teaching research subjects Conduct Learning Action Cell (LAC) sessions on the use of the different learning resources Intensive monitoring and evaluation to research teachers	SHS Research Teachers, School Heads, Department Heads Resource Speakers	YEAR 1 J F M A M J J A S O N D	Php 50,000.00 Source of Fund: MOOE / Canteen Fund	80 – 100% of the SHS research teachers shall have attended trainings on methodologies in teaching research.
	To assist research teachers in publishing their research outputs To instill upon teachers the relevance of publications	Create links with research publications Conduct seminars on how to publish research works. Establish connections/tie-up with organizations on research and agencies	SHS Research Teachers, Resource Speakers, School Heads, Department Heads, Heads of Funding Agencies, Heads of Public and Private Publication Companies, Heads of Research Education Institutions,	YEAR 3 J F M A M J J A S O N D	Php 100,000.00 Source of Fund: MOOE / Canteen Fund	75% of the SHS research teachers shall have published their research works

Areas of Concern	Objectives	Strategies	Persons and Agencies Involved	Time Frame	Budgetary Requirements	Expected Outcomes
	To boost the teachers' willingness to network with other research organizations and agencies	such as Department of Science and Technology (DOST) Encourage all research teachers to conduct personal researches	SDS, ASDS, Chiefs of CID and SGOD			
	To upgrade the research teachers' skills on how to apply and disseminate research studies	Establish networking with research organizations	SHS Research Teachers, Resource Speakers, School Heads, Department Heads, Heads of Funding Agencies, Heads of Public and Private Publication Companies, Heads of Research Education Institutions, SDS, ASDS, Chiefs of CID and SGOD	YEAR 3 J F M A M J J A S O N D	Php 100,000.00 Source of Fund: MOOE / Canteen Fund	75% of the SHS research teachers shall have disseminated and applied their published research studies.

Areas of Concern	Objectives	Strategies	Persons and Agencies Involved	Time Frame	Budgetary Requirements	Expected Outcomes
B. Delivery of Instruction ***1. Research Content and Pedagogy***	To fortify skills and competencies of teachers in the delivery of instruction along research	Create a monthly Focus Group Discussions as an avenue for sharing research teaching strategies and techniques Provide intensive trainings, fora, workshops, lectures, symposia and LAC Sessions on how to plan, organize, and implement educational research Provide seminars on inquiry-based approach, contextualization, scientific methods, and HOTS and how they are integrated in research subjects Enroll in graduate school courses for the upskilling of research skills	SHS Research Teachers, School Heads, Department Heads	**YEAR 1** J F M A M J J A S O N D	Php 150,000.00 Source of Fund: MOOE / Canteen Fund	At least 80% of the SHS research teachers have improved teaching strategies and techniques as well as improved knowledge, skills, and understanding in educational research.

Areas of Concern	Objectives	Strategies	Persons and Agencies Involved	Time Frame	Budgetary Requirements	Expected Outcomes
2. Mentoring and Collaboration	To provide teachers the opportunities to share their experiences in going through research with colleagues and students as well	Provide team building activities among SHS research teachers and students to establish good rapport between and among them Assign SHS Research Teachers, especially Master Teachers, as research focal person in the department Schedule teachers with mentoring sessions with students and colleague Allow students to join online Investigatory Project Contest	SHS Research Teachers, School Heads, Department Heads, Resource Speakers	YEAR 1 J F M A M J J A S O N D	Php 100,000.00 Source of Fund: MOOE / Canteen Fund	At least 75% of the SHS research teachers participated in the team building activities and conducted mentoring activities with the learners and colleagues.
3. Budget	To provide financial support in research engagement	Appropriate sufficient funding to finance the needs of SHS research teachers in fulfilling their duties as research advocates	SHS Research Teachers, School Heads, Department Heads	YEAR ROUND J F M A M J J A S O N D	Php 200,000.00 Source of Fund: MOOE / Local School Board Fund	At least 75% of the schools have funds that support the activities of the SHS research teachers.

Areas of Concern	Objectives	Strategies	Persons and Agencies Involved	Time Frame	Budgetary Requirements	Expected Outcomes
4. Availability of research journals, books, and references	To update library resources	Purchase additional and relevant textbooks and reference books Establish tie-up among other schools or higher educational institutions for the sharing of resources Create a MOA with the Provincial, City and Municipal Libraries Utilize the I-hub as a learning resource center Request books and other supplementary materials from alumni and other civic-spirited citizens	SHS Research Teachers, School Heads, Department Heads, Administrative Officers, Head of the Higher Educational Institution, Provincial, City, and Municipal Officials, Alumni, Civic-Spirited Citizens	YEAR ROUND J F M A M J J A S O N D	Php 500,000.00 Source of Fund: MOOE / Donations / LGU / NGO	At least 75% of the teachers and students' needs on research resources were provided.
5. Time	To provide teachers adequate time to do research	Provide proper scheduling of workloads to give them time to prepare their research and conduct mentoring sessions	SHS Research Teachers, School Heads, Department Heads	YEAR 1 J F M A M J J A S O N D		100% of the SHS research teachers have improved working schedules

Areas of Concern	Objectives	Strategies	Persons and Agencies Involved	Time Frame	Budgetary Requirements	Expected Outcomes
6. Volume of school work and other work-related activities	To reduce teaching workload to pave way for research activities	Remove the other workloads of SHS research teachers and give priority to their research skill development	SHS Research Teachers, School Heads, Department Heads	YEAR 1 J F M A M J J A S O N D		100% of the SHS research teachers are given appropriate workloads
7. Class size	To provide ample time to teachers in monitoring their students	Monitor the distribution of the students in every section	SHS Research Teachers, School Heads, Department Heads, Provincial, City, and Municipal Officials	YEAR 1 J F M A M J J A S O N D		100% of the SHS research teachers have improved class sizes.
8. Qualifications of research teachers	To upgrade the qualifications of teachers in research	Request funds from the PSB/*Sagip Guro* Program Assign teachers are really capable of teaching SHS research subjects	SHS Research Teachers, School Heads, Department Heads.	YEAR 1 J F M A M J J A S O N D	Php 200,000.00 Source of Fund: Local School Board Fund	100% of the SHS research teachers are qualified to teach SHS research teachers.
9. Access to internet and other online resources	To furnish teachers with ICT related equipments and increase their skills on the use of technology	Avail of the different ICT initiatives of the different school divisions in the province such as the use of the Rachel Pi	SHS Research Teachers, School Heads, Department Heads, Division Office ICT	YEAR ROUND J F M A M J J A S O N D	Php 500,000.00 Source of Fund: MOOE / LGU / NGO	100% of the SHS research teachers have access to internet and other online materials.

Areas of Concern	Objectives	Strategies	Persons and Agencies Involved	Time Frame	Budgetary Requirements	Expected Outcomes
10. Availability of computers, printers, and other equipment		Apply for faster internet speed connections from service providers Purchase additional computers, printers, and other equipment Solicit from the LGU, NGO, alumni, and other civic spirited citizens	Coordinators, Internet Service Providers SHS Research Teachers, School Heads, Department Heads, Private Companies, LGU, NGO, Alumni, Civic-spirited citizen	YEAR 1 J F M A M J J A S O N D	Php 500,000.00 Source of Fund: MOOE / Donations / LGU / NGO	100% of the SHS research teachers have computers, printers, and other equipment provided by the school.
C. Professional Advancements	To upgrade the educational qualifications of SHS research teachers by encouraging them to finish their masters or doctorate degrees	Provide any of the following • Study leave grants • Scholarship grant Create a teacher development fund to serve as soft loan for graduate studies	SHS Research Teachers. School Heads, Human Resource Development Officer	YEAR ROUND J F M A M J J A S O N D	Php 500,000.00 Source of Fund: Canteen Fund	30% to 50% of the SHS Research Teachers have completed their masters and doctorate degrees.

Areas of Concern	Objectives	Strategies	Persons and Agencies Involved	Time Frame	Budgetary Requirements	Expected Outcomes
		Develop an incentive program for making research publications Provide lecture/seminar on grammar rules in English Conduct seminar-workshop on creative and technical writing Provide intensive training on research preparation, implementation, and reporting Assign SHS Research Teachers, especially Master Teachers, as research focal person in the department Create Focus Group Discussions for possible group action research	CID and SGOD			

Areas of Concern	Objectives	Strategies	Persons and Agencies Involved	Time Frame	Budgetary Requirements	Expected Outcomes
		Establish partnership with research education institution Enroll in graduate school courses for the upskilling of research skills				

2. Experts' Perceptions of the Upskilling Program for SHS Research Teachers

"The program presents comprehensive and attainable activities that are relevant to the needs of the SHS research teachers."

Joye D. Madalipay EdD
Assistant Schools Division Superintendent
Schools Division of Ilocos Norte

"The program highlights the importance of linkages and partnerships which are vital factors in doing researches."

Elsie C. Pilar EdD
Dean, College of Teacher Education
Northwestern University
Laoag City

"It is worthy to note that the program recognizes the noble roles played by different individuals in the conduct of a research study."

Aris Reynold V. Cajigal PhD
Dean, College of Teacher Education
Mariano Marcos State University
Laoag City

"The Upskilling Program for SHS Research Teachers will be a great help in attainment of quality education in the country."

Rajah Adib G. Reyes EdD
SHS Master Teacher II
Dingras National High School
Dingras, Ilocos Norte

"The program is timely and relevant. It is needs-based. It could be a great help if implemented. Congratulations!

Eldefonso B. Natividad Jr. PhD
Education Program Supervisor
Schools Division of Batac City

"The program will really cater the needs of the SHS research teachers. Good job!"

Erick Medrano
Senior Education Program Specialist for Research
Schools Division of Ilocos Norte

3. 10 Tips to Improve the Philippine Education Research Curriculum

1. Research teachers who are non-education graduates are encouraged to take professional education courses and attend graduate studies to improve their skills and competencies.
2. School administrators should send their teachers to research-related trainings for them to be equipped with the needed skills in teaching the research subjects assigned to them.
3. School administrators should provide the needed facilities or financial resources needed in the implementation of the research curriculum and see to it that the problems encountered by the teachers be addressed.
4. A support system should be created by the school heads or DepEd officials so that research teachers can communicate their concerns with their colleagues, share their ideas, and collectively provide solutions to emerging problems in teaching research. This can be established by forming a

professional organization of SHS research teachers within a division or in a wider geographical scope.

5. Technical assistance should be extended by the school heads to their teachers. This can be reflected by devising a clear monitoring and mentoring plan to keep track of and verify the improvement of the research teachers on their role as research teachers and researchers in their respective schools.
6. SHS research teachers with highly proficient level of competence should be tapped as resource speakers, facilitators, mentors, or organizers in relevant trainings to improve the competencies of other research teachers which will be delivered in their respective departments, schools, or divisions. In effect, research teachers are given opportunity to sustain their level of competence while providing instructional support to their colleagues.
7. Copies of the Upskilling Program should be provided by the researcher to the school administrators, program heads, and human resource divisions for possible adoption as a basis in providing competency-based trainings for the enhancement of research teachers' skills, knowledge, and understanding.

8. For the initial implementation of the crafted training design, the school administrators are encouraged to adopt the prepared training matrix for the enhancement of research teachers.
9. Research teachers are encouraged to conduct their own researches as an application of the program. A system of evaluating their research outputs must be devised.
10. Implementation of the Upskilling Program for SHS Research Teachers.

About the Author

Dr. Sherwin Jay Prado Palaspas is currently a Senior High School Master Teacher II of San Nicolas National High School, San Nicolas, Ilocos Norte.

He graduated Cum Laude with the degree Bachelor in Secondary Education major in Chemistry at the Mariano Marcos State University - College of Teacher Education, Laoag City, finished his Master of Arts in Education major in General Science and Doctor in Education major in Educational Management at the Northwestern University's Vedasto J. Samonte School of Graduate Studies, Laoag City.

He is an award winning research and science coach, seasoned speaker in research and science forums and seminars, and a foreign language teacher in Mandarin.

Bibliography

Published/Unpublished Materials

Adebayo, F.A. & Sagaya, A.A. (2015). *Teachers' capacity building and students' academic performance among public junior secondary schools in Kwara State.* British Journal of Education, Society & Behavioral Science, 12(3), 1-10.

Alexandrou, A. & Swaffield, S. (2014). *Teacher leadership and professional development.* Abingdon: Routledge.

Almeida, A. B. (2016). *Research Fundamentals From Concept to Output.* Manila: Adriana Printing Co., Inc.

Aminudin, N.A. (2012). *Teachers' perceptions of the impact of professional development on teaching practice: The case of one primary school.* Master's Degree Thesis. Unitec Institute of Technology.

Anderson, R.D. (2007). *Inquiry as an organisng theme for science curricula.* Handbook of Research on Science Education. New York: Routledge.

Bagaoisan, M. (2018). *Benchmarking the practices of the centers of technical excellence: Basis of a development framework for technical-vocational schools in Ilocos Norte.* Unpublished Dissertation. Divine Word College of Laoag, Graduate School, Laoag City, Philippines.

Birky, V. D., Shelton, M., & Headley, S. (2006). *An administrator's challenge: Encouraging teachers to be leaders.* NASSP Bulletin, 90(2), 87–101.

Borko, H. (2014). *Professional development and teacher learning: Mapping the terrain.* Educational Researcher, 33(8), 3–15.

Bryk, A. S., Sebring, P. B., Allensworth, E., Luppescu, S., & Easton, J. Q. (2010). *Organizing schools for improvement: Lessons from Chicago.* Chicago, IL: University of Chicago Press.

Cabanatan, R. A. (2010). *Competencies of Physics Teachers.* Research Proposal. Mariano Marcos State University. Graduate School, Laoag City, Philippines.

Carles, D.R. (1997). *Managing Systematic Curriculum Change: A Critical Analysis of Hongkong's Target-Oriented Curriculum Initiative.* International Review of Education, 43 (4), 349-366.

Cudapas, E. V. (2019). *Action Research Handbook for Mathematics Teachers*. Unpublished Dissertation. Divine Word College of Laoag, Graduate School, Laoag City, Philippines.

Darling-Hammond, L. (2010). *Professional learning in the learning profession: A status report on teacher development in the United States and abroad.* Oxford, OH: National Staff Development Council.

Darling-Hammond, L., Chung, R. W., Andree, A., & Richardson, N. (2009). *Professional learning in the learning profession: A status report on teacher development in the United States and abroad.* Oxford, OH: National Staff Development Council.

Dobie, T. E. & Anderson, E. R. (2015). *Interaction in teacher communities: Three forms teachers use to express contrasting ideas in video clubs.* Teaching and Teacher Education, 47, 230–240.

DuFour, R. & Fullan, M. (2012). *Cultures built to last: Systemic PLCs at work.* Bloomington, IN: Solution Tree Press.

Ebert, E. & Culyer R. (2012). *An Introduction to Education.* Cengage Advantage Books. United States of America.

Ellis, N. & Loughland, T. (2016). *The challenges of practitioner research: A comparative study of Singapore and NSW.* Australian Journal of Teacher Education, 41(2), 121-136.

Ermeling, B. A. & Yarbo, J. (2016). *Expanding instructional horizons: A case study of teacher team-outside expert partnership.* Teachers Colleges Record, 118(2), 1–48.

Faltado, R. E. (2016). *Practical Research 2 Quantitative Research.* Manila: Lorimar Publishing, Inc.

Fullan, M.G. (2007). *Successful School Improvement: The Implementation Perspective and Beyond.* Milton Keynes: Open University Press.

Gardner, A.L. & Gess-Newsome, J. (2011). *A PCK rubric to measure teachers' knowledge of inquiry-based instruction using three data sources.* Orlando, FL.

Grande, R. N. (2015). *Outcomes-Based Education for Colleges of Nursing in the Philippines.* Unpublished Dissertation. Mariano Marcos State University, Graduate School, Laoag City, Philippines.

Jones, M. & Carter, G. (2007). *Science teacher attitudes and beliefs.* Handbook of research on science education. New York: Routledge.

Lewis, J. M., Fischman, D., Riggs, I., & Wasserman, K. (2013). *Teacher learning in lesson study.* The Mathematics Enthusiast, 10(3), 583–620.

Lewthwaite, B. (2001). *The development, validation and application of a primary science curriculum implementation questionnaire.* Unpublished ScEdD Thesis, Curtin University of Technology, Perth.

Lewthwaite, B. (2006). *"I want to enable teachers in their change": Exploring the role of a superintendent on science curriculum delivery.* Canadian Journal of educational Administration and Policy, 52, 1-24.

Lewthwaite, B.E, Stableford, J. & Fisher, D.L. (2010). *Enlarging the focus on primary science education in New Zealand.* In R.K Coll (Ed.) SAMEpapers 2001 (213-237).

Little, J. W. (2012). *Professional community and professional development in the learning-centered school.* London: Routledge.

Lynch, D. (2002). *Professor should embrace technology in courses.* Chronicle of Higher Education, B15.

Luft, J.A. & Hewson, P.W. (2014). *Research on teacher professional development programs in science.* Handbook of Research in Science Education. New York: Routledge.Magopeni.

MacBeath, J. & Dempster, N. (2008). *Connecting leadership and learning. Principles for practice.* London: Routledge.

Natividad, E.B. (2018). *Capability Enhancement Framework in Mathematics for Secondary School Master Teachers.* Unpublished Disseration. Divine Word College of Laoag, Graduate School, Laoag City, Philippines.

Ortal, J.R. (2018). *Achievement Motivation, work attitudes and performance of master teachers: Bases for the development of a capability enhancement program.* Unpublished Dissertation: Northwestern University, Graduate School, Laoag City, Philippines.

Othman, N. & Chia, S.Y. (2016). *The challenges of action research implementation in Malaysian schools.* Pertanika Journal of Social Sciences and Humanities, 24(1), 43-52.

Pati, P. (2014). *Indonesian foreign school teachers' perception and capability to undertake classroom action research: Basis for capability building program.* IOSR Journal of Research & Method in Education, 4(1), 67-89.

Puso, V. (2013). *A proposed training design on enhancing research capabilities of teachers, master teachers, and school heads in the Division of City Schools, Iriga City.*

Ramnarain, U. & Fortus, D. (2013). *South African physical sciences teachers' perceptions of new content in a revised curriculum.* South African Journal of Education, 33(1), 1-15.

Rennie, L.J. (2001). *Teacher Collaboration in Curriculum Change: The Implementation of Technology Education in the Primary School.* Research in Science Education, 31, 49-69.

Reyes, R.G. (2019). *Implementation of the Science Education Curriculum in the Public Senior High Schools of Ilocos Norte.* Unpublished Dissertation. Mariano Marcos State University, Graduate School, Laoag City, Philippines.

Rogan, J.M. & Grayson, D.J. (2003). *Towards a theory of curriculum implementation with particular reference to science education in developing countries.* International Journal of Science Education, 25(10), 1171-1204.

Sade, D. & Coll, R.K. (2003). *Technology and Technology Education: Views of Some Solomon Island Primary Teachers and Curriculum Development Officers.* International Journal of Science and Mathematics Education, 1, 87-114.

Science Education Institute. (2011). *Framework for Philippine Mathematics Teacher Education.* Manila: SEI-DOST & MATHED.

Salazar, F. R. (2020). *School Funding.* Manila. Phoenix Publishing House.

Timperley, H. (2011). *Realizing the power of professional learning.* London: McGraw-Hill Education.

Tindowen, D. J., Guzman, J., & Macanang, D. (2019). *Teachers' conception and difficulties in doing action research.* Universal Journal of Educational Research, 7(8), 1787-1794.

Ulla, M. B. (2017). *Benefits and challenges of doing research: Experiences from Philippine public school teachers.* Issues in Educational Research, 28(3), 797-810.

United Nations Educational, Scientific and Cultural Organization. (2011). *UNESCO ICT Competency Framework for Teachers.* Paris, France: UNESCO.

Wang, Y.C. (2006). *Capability building model for secondary mathematics teachers.* The Journal of Human Resource and Adult Learning, 23-33.

World Bank. (2016). *Developing a proficient and motivated teacher workforce in the Philippines.* Philippine Education Note, No.10.

Zhou, R. N. (2012). *Importance of Research.* China: Hou Va Printing Factory.

Online Sources

Alda, R. (2020). *Teacher Education Institutions in the Philippines towards Education 4.0.* Retrieved from: https://www.ijlter.org/index.php/ijlter/article/view/2449. Date Accessed: December 5, 2020.

Alkhahtani, A. (2017). *The challenges facing the integration of ICT in teaching in Saudi secondary schools.* Retrieved from: https://files.eric.ed.gov/fulltext/EJ1142266.pdf. Date Accessed: December 5, 2020.

Andrew, M.M. (2015). *Teacher Characteristics.* Retrieved from: https://cees.uonbi.ac.ke/sites/default/files/cees/VIMTECH%20FINAL%202-hard%20copy_0.pdf. Date Accessed: March 15, 2020.

Andriotis, N. (2017). *Upskilling Employees: Advantages and Methods To Teach Staff More.* Retrieved from: https://www.efrontlearning.com/blog/2017/05/upskilling-training-employees-advantages-methods.html.
Date Accessed: June 4, 2020.

Ciriaco, C.M. (2019). *DepEd vows to improve quality of education after PISA showing.* Retrieved from: https://businessmirror.com.ph. Date Accessed: March 14, 2020.

Department of Education. *DepEd Order No. 1, s. 2020.* Retrieved from: deped.gov.ph/2020/01/23/january-23-2020-do-001-s-2020-guidelines-for-neap-recognition-of-professional-development-programs-and-courses-for-teachers-and-school-leaders/. Date Accessed: March 7, 2020.

Department of Education. *DepEd Order No. 35, s. 2016.* Retrieved from: deped.gov.ph/2016/06/07/do-35-s-2016-the-learning-action-cell-as-a-k-to-12-basic-education-program-school-based-continuing-professional-development-strategy-for-the-improvement-of-teaching-and-learning/. Date Accessed: March 7, 2020.

Department of Education. *DepEd Order No. 3, s. 2016.* Retrieved from: deped.gov.ph/2016/01/21/do-3-s-2016-hiring-guidelines-for-senior-high-school-shs-teaching-positions-effective-school-year-sy-2016-2017/. Date Accessed: March 7, 2020.

Department of Education. *Inquiries, Investigation, and Immersion Curriculum Guide.* Retrieved from: https://www.deped.gov.ph/wp-content/uploads/ 2019/01/SHS-Applied_Inquiries-Investigations-and-Immersions-CG.pdf. Date Accessed: March 7, 2020.

Department of Education. *Practical Research 1 Curriculum Guide.* Retrieved from: https://www.deped.gov.ph/wp-content/uploads/2019/01/SHS-Applied_Research-1-CG.pdf. Date Accessed: March 7, 2020.

Department of Education. *Practical Research 2 Curriculum Guide.* Retrieved from: https://www.deped.gov.ph/wp-content/uploads/2019/01/SHS-Applied_Research-2-CG.pdf. Date Accessed: March 7, 2020.

Department of Education. *Primer on the New K-12 Philippine Education Curriculum.* Retrieved from http://www.smartparenting.com.ph/ kids/preschooler/k-12-101-a-primer-on-the-new-philippine-education-curriculum. Date Accessed. March 14, 2020.

Department of Education. *Research.* Retrieved from: https://www.deped.gov. ph/wp-content/uploads/2019/01/Research.pdf. Date Accessed: March 7, 2020.

Dunne, K. A. (2012). *Teachers as Learners: Elements of Effective Professional Development.* Retrieved from: https://images.pearsonassessments. com/images/NES_Publications/2012_08Dunne_475_1.pdf. Date Accessed: March 15, 2020.

Ellis N. & Loughland, T. (2016). *The Challenges of Practitioner Research: A Comparative Study of Singapore and NSW*. Retrived from: https://www.researchgate.net/publication/295830556_The_Challengesof_Practitioner_Research_A_Comparative_Study_of_Singapore_and_NSW. Date Accessed: March 15, 2020.

Finger, G. (2006). *The implementation of technology education: intrinsic and extrinsic challenges for queensland teachers.* Retrieved from: https://www.researchgate.net/publication/29461878_The_implementation_of_Technology_Education_Intrinsic_and_extrinsic_challenges_for_Queensland_teachers. Date Accessed: March 15, 2020.

Firdissa, J. A. (2015). *Motivating and/or de-motivating environments to do action research: the case of teachers of English as a foreign language in Ethiopian universities.* Retrieved from: https://www.tandfonline.com/ doi/abs/10.1080/09650792.2016.1168310?af=R&journalCode=reac20. Date Accessed: March 15, 2020.

Flumerfelt, S., & Green, G. (2013). *Using Lean in the flipped classroom for at risk students.* Educational Technology & Society. Retrieved from: http://www.ifets.info/journals/16_1/31.pdf. Date Accessed: March 15, 2020.

Garet, M. et.al. (2001). *What Makes Professional Development Effective?* Retrieved from: https://journals.sagepub.com/doi/abs/10.3102/000283 12038004915?journalCode=aera. Date Accessed: March 15, 2020.

Gomez, M. S. & Panaligan, C. (2013). *Level of research competencies and satisfaction of the faculty members from the College of Criminology.* Retrieved from: http://research.lpubatangas.edu.ph/wp-content/uploads/2014/04/AARJSH-LEVEL-OF-RESEARCH-COMPETENCIES-AND-SATISFACTION-OF-THE.pdf. Date Accessed: April 1, 2020.

Gordon, E. (2019). *Curriculum Quality Rubrics: A Self-Assessment Tool for Districts.* Retrieved from: https://www.cgcs.org/cms/lib/DC00001581/ Centricity/Domain/4/Curriculum%20Quality%20Rubric.pdf. Date Accessed: June 2, 2020.

Gorenflo, G. & Moran, J. W. (2010). *The ABCs of PDCA.* Retrieved from: http://www. phf.org/nphpsp/ViewResourceLink.aspx?source= http%3a%2f%2fwww.phf.org%2fresourcestools%2fPages%2 f The_ABCs_of__PDCA.aspx&title=The+ABCs+of+PDCA. Date Accessed: March 15, 2020.

Gray, Crawford (2007). Research Competencies Framework. Retrieved from: https://www.fgdp.org.uk/sites/fgdp.org.uk/files/docs/in-practice/Research/research%20competencies.pdf. Date Accessed: March 20, 2020

Gregson, J. & Sturko, P. (2007). *Teachers as Adult Learners: Re-conceptualizing Professional Development.* Retrieved from: https://files.eric.ed.gov/fulltext/EJ891061.pdf. Date Accessed: March 15, 2020.

Haciomeroglu, G. (2017). *Reciprocal relationships between mathematics anxiety and attitude towards mathematics in elementary students.* Retrieved from: https://files.eric.ed.gov/fulltext/EJ1160567.pdf. Date Accessed: March 15, 2020.

Hermans, R. (2010*). Taking Prospective Teachers' Beliefs into Account in Teacher Education.* Retrieved from: https://www.researchgate.net/publication/279616532. Date Accessed: March 15, 2020.

Hoeschl, M. B., Bueno, T. C., & Hoeschl, H. C. (2017). *Fourth industrial revolution and the future of engineering: could robots replace human jobs? How ethical recommendations can help engineers rule on artificial intelligence*. Retrieved from: https://doi.org/10.1109/weef.2017.8466973. Date Accessed: March 15, 2020.

Kangori, B.N. (2014). *Teacher-Related Factor.* Retrieved from: https://cees.uonbi.ac.ke/sites/default/files/cees/BRIGID%20N.%20KANGORI%20FINAL%20PROJECT.pdf. Date Accessed: March 15, 2020.

Kho, M. & Ling, Y. (2017). *A Study of Perception and Capability to Undertake Action Research Among Lecturers at a Polytechnic in Sarawa.* Retrieved from: https://www.researchgate.net/publication/318876686. Date Accessed: December 5, 2020.

Kotter, J.P. (2006). *Leading Change Why Transformation Efforts Fail.* Retrieved from: https://www.lifelongfaith.com/uploads/5/1/6/4/5164069/leading_change_-_kotter.pdf. Date Accessed: March 15, 2020.

Lipsey, M., Rossi P., & Freeman, H (2003). *Evaluation: A Systematic Approach.* 7th Ed. SAGE Publications. Retrieved from: https://www.slideshare.net/israelvc12/evaluation-a-systematic -approachrossilipseyfreeman. Date Accessed: March 15, 2020.

Magpayo, C. (2015). *Grammatical Competence of First Year English Major Students of Teacher Education Department in Holy Angel University A.Y. 2014-2015: An Assessment.* Retrieved from: academia.edu/36609309/Grammatical_Competence_of_First_Year_English_Major_Students_of_Teacher_Education_Department_in_Holy_Angel_University_A_Y_2014_2015_An_Assessment. Date Accessed: December 5, 2020.

Mandukwini, N. (2016). *Challenges towards curriculum.* Retrieved from:https://core.ac.uk/download/pdf/83637231.pdf. Date Accessed: March 15, 2020.

Manongsong, M. G. & Panopio, E. (2018). *Dentistry faculty members' research competencies and attitude towards research engagement.* Retrieved from: www.apjeas.apjmr.com. Date Accessed: March 20, 2020.

Mergler, A. & Spooner, R. (2012). What Pre-service Teachers Need to Know to be Effective at Values-based Education. Retrieved from: https://files.eric.ed.gov/fulltext/EJ995221.pdf. Date Accessed: November 20, 2020.

Millard, M. (2018). *6 Principles of the Continuous Improvement Model.* Retrieved from: https://blog.kainexus.com/continuous-improvement/6-principles-of-the-continuous-improvement-model. Date Accessed: March 15, 2020.

Miscovic, M. et.al. (2012). Action Research in Action: From University to School Classrooms. Retrieved from: https://www.researchgate.net/publication/258384214_Action_Research_in_Action_From_University_to_School_Classrooms. Date Accessed: December 5, 2020.

Nolasco, R. (2010). The Prospects Of Multilingual Education And Literacy In The Philippines. Retrieved from: https://www.seameo.org/_ld2008/doucments/Presentation_document/NolascoTHE_PROSPECTS_OF_MULTILINGUAL_EDUCATION.pdf. Date Accessed: December 5, 2020.

Orey, M. (2010). *Emerging Perspectives on Learning, Teaching, and Technology.* Retrieved from: https://textbookequity.org/Textbooks/Orey_Emergin_Perspectives_Learning.pdf. Date Accessed: March 15, 2020.

Park, S. et.al. (2013). *Continuous Improvement in education.* Retrieved from: https://www.carnegiefoundation.org/wp-content/uploads/2014/09/carnegie-foundation_continuous-improvement_2013.05.pdf. Date Accessed: March 15, 2020.

Postholm, M.B. (2018). *Teachers professional development in school.* Retrieved from: https://www.tandfonline.com/doi/full/10.1080/2331186X.2018.1522781. Date Accessed: March 7, 2020.

Pratseyo, A. P. (2010). *Learning Paradigm of biology teaching, educational background, school culture, perception, attitude, intrinsic motivation, metacognitive awareness*. Retrieved from: pasca.um.ac.id/..../5-colletion-abstractBIO-S3-2. Date Accessed: March 7, 2020.

President's Management Agenda (2019). *Reskilling Toolkit.* Retrieved from: https://www.opm.gov/policy-data-oversight/workforce restructuring/ reshaping/accelerating-the-gears-of-transformation/reskilling-toolkit.pdf. Date Accessed: June 4, 2020.

Ramnarain, U. (2016). *Understanding the influence of intrinsic and extrinsic factors on inquiry-based science education at township schools in South Africa.* Retrieved from: https://www.researchgate.net/publication/ 293194203 Understanding_the_influence_of_intrinsic_and_extrinsic_ factors_on_inquirybased_science_education at_township_schools_ in_South_Africa. Date Accessed: March 15, 2020.

Sali-ot, M. (2019). *Competencies of Instructors: Its Correlation to the Factors Affecting the Academic Performance of Students.* Retrieved from: https://ejournals.ph/article.php?id=7468. Date Accessed: December 5, 2020.

Schartz, M. S. & Sadler, P. M. (2019). Empowerment in Science Curriculum Development: A Microdevelopmental Approach. Retrieved from: https://www.researchgate.net/publication/248974471_Empowerment_inScience_Curriculum_Development_A_microdevelopmental_approach. Date Accessed: March 15, 2020.

Sheikh, A.S.F., Sheikh, S.A., Kaleem, A., Waqas, A. (2013). *Factors contributing to lack of interest in research among medical students.* Retrieved from: https://www.dovepress.com/factors-contributing-to-lack-of-interest-in-research-among-medical-stu-peer-reviewed-article-AMEP. Date Accessed: December 5, 2020.

Sleeter, O. (2008). *A Study on Chemistry in the Philippines.* Retrieved from: http://www.wikipedia.com/chem. Date Accessed: March 7, 2020.

Smith, G. & Yates, P. (2011). *Team Role Theory in Higher Education.* Retrieved from: https://www.belbin.com/media/1819/tj-article-team-role-theory-in-higher-education.pdf. Date Accessed: March 7, 2020.

Steyn, G. M. (2008). *Continuing professional development for teachers in South Africa and social learning systems: conflicting conceptual frameworks of learning.* Retrieved from: http://www.scielo.org.za/pdf/koers/v73n1/02.pdf. Date Accessed: March 15, 2020.

Swindoll, C. R. (2012). *Senior High School Students' Attitudes Towards Research.* Retrieved from: https://papers.ssrn.com/sol3/papers.cfm?abstract_id=3263496. Date Accessed: March 15, 2020.

Taflinger R. E. (2011). *Introduction to Research.* Retrieved from: https://public.wsu.edu/~taflinge/research.html. Date Accessed.
March 15, 2020.

Terrada, Y. (2017). *The Case for Mentors Grows Stronger.* Retrieved from: https://www.edutopia.org/article/case-mentors-grows-stronger-youki-terada#:~:text=Providing%20high%2Dquality%20mentors%20to,students%2C%20a%20new%20study%20finds.&text=Past%20research%20has%20shown%20that,out%20and%20leaving%20the%20profession. Date Accessed: March 5, 2020.

Ulla, M. B. (2017). *Philippine Classroom Teachers as Researchers: Teachers' Perceptions, Motivations, and Challenges.* Retrieved from: https://files.eric.ed.gov/fulltext/EJ1161165.pdf. Date Accessed: March 5, 2020.

Valente, M.O. (2015). *The process of teacher change as a consequence of professional development .* Retrieved from: https://www.researchgate.net/publication/280569379. Date Accessed: March 15, 2020.

Vandeyar, S. (2017). *The Teacher as an Agent of Meaningful Educational Change.* Retrieved from: https://files.eric.ed.gov/fulltext/EJ1147491.pdf Date Accessed: March 15, 2020.

Vasquez, V. E. (2017). *Teachers as researchers: Advantages, disadvantages and challenges for teachers intending to engage in research activities.* Retrieved from: https://www.academia.edu/719736. Date Accessed: March 20, 2020

Wa-Mbaleka, S. (2015). *Feature Factors Leading to Limited Faculty Publications in Philippine Higher Education Institutions.* Retrieved from: https://www.researchgate.net/publication/290395664_Factors_Leading_to_Limited_Faculty_Publications_in_Philippine_Higher_Education_Institutions#:~:text=Findings%20reveal%20that%20the%207,and%20lack%20of%20institutional%20support. Date Accessed: March 5, 2020.

Wong, A. (2019). *Driving Forces Of Master Teachers' Research Capability: Towards Building A Research Culture In The Division Of Romblon, Philippines.* Retrieved from: http://www.ijarp.org/published-research-papers/july2019/Driving-Forces-Of-Master-Teachers-Research-Capability-Towards-Building-A-Research-Culture-In-The-Division-Of-Romblon-Philippines.pdf. Date Accessed: March 5, 2020.

Yoon, K. S., Campbell, M. P., &. Sztajn, P. (2011). *Conceptualizing professional development in mathematics: elements of a model.* Retrieved from: https://www.researchgate.net/publication/49912216_Conceptualizing_professional_development_in_mathematics_Elements_of_a_model. Date Accessed: March 15, 2020.

__________________ (2020). *Continuous Improvement.* Retrieved from: https://www.edglossary.org/continuous-improvement/. Date Accessed: March 20, 2020

_________________ (2011). *Educational Research.* Retrieved from: http://www.termpaperwarehouse.com/essayon/The_Importa nce_
Of_Educational Research. Date Accessed: March 18, 2020

_________________ (2020). *Importance of Research.* Retrieved from: (http://www.uniteforsight.org). Date Accessed: March 20, 2020

_________________ (2011). *The Importance of Educational Research.* Retrieved from: http://www.termpaperwarehouse.com/essay on/The_Importance_Of_Educational Research. Date Accessed: March 20, 2020

www.ingramcontent.com/pod-product-compliance
Ingram Content Group UK Ltd.
Pitfield, Milton Keynes, MK11 3LW, UK
UKHW061828190726
13853UKWH00009B/2488